THE EMPOWERED
empath

chartwell
books

© 2024 Quarto Publishing Group USA Inc.

This edition published in 2024 by Chartwell Books,
an imprint of The Quarto Group
142 West 36th Street, 4th Floor
New York, NY 10018 USA
T (212) 779-4972 F (212) 779-6058
www.Quarto.com

10 9 8 7 6 5 4 3 2 1

Chartwell titles are also available at discount for retail, wholesale, promotional, and
bulk purchase. For details, contact the Special Sales Manager by email at
specialsales@quarto.com or by mail at The Quarto Group, Attn: Special Sales Manager,
100 Cummings Center Suite 265D, Beverly, MA 01915, USA.

ISBN: 978-0-7858-4471-6

Publisher: Wendy Friedman
Publishing Director: Meredith Mennitt
Editor: Jennifer Kushnier
Cover Designer: Kate Sinclair
Designer: Angelika Piwowarczyk

All stock photos and design elements ©Shutterstock

Printed in China

This book provides general information. It should not be relied upon as recommending
or promoting any specific diagnosis or method of treatment for a particular condition.
It is not intended as a substitute for medical advice or for direct diagnosis and
treatment of a medical or psychological condition by a qualified physician or therapist.
Readers who have questions about a particular condition, possible treatments for that
condition, or possible reactions from the condition or its treatment should consult a
physician, therapist, or other qualified healthcare professional.

THE
EMPOWERED
empath

A WORKBOOK TO HELP
HIGHLY SENSITIVE PEOPLE SET
BOUNDARIES, LEARN SELF-RELIANCE,
AND PROTECT THEIR SPIRIT

SUSAN REYNOLDS

chartwell
books

Contents

INTRODUCTION

Empathy is the ability to listen, understand, and care so deeply about other human beings that you can sense what it's like to be them. It's an essential relationship skill. Unfortunately, in our fast-paced, super-stressed, narrowly focused lives, not enough people feel empathy for their fellow human beings—not enough people, that is, except for those who are *empaths*.

Empaths' sensitivity and intuition are so finely tuned they not only *feel compassion* for others, but they also *take on the feelings* of those around them, as if the emotions were their own. While it may sound noble—and it can be, when managed and balanced—many empaths have difficulty setting and maintaining boundaries. And when you live your life so open to feeling other people's emotional pain that you feel what they feel, you often don't have enough energy to manage your own life and begin to put your own needs on hold. Empaths tend to neglect themselves, and over time, may feel so drained, they use ineffective coping methods, hampering their ability to live their best life.

This book is designed to help empaths and highly sensitive people, particularly those in need of healing, discover where they've gone wrong and what they can do to rein in their tendences to give, give, give, so they can focus on themselves and what they most need.

We'll first define what it means to be an empath, and then help you determine if you're in *hyper*-empath mode or suffering from empath fatigue. As you likely are, we'll walk through strategies for healing and rebuilding, including how to identify your vulnerabilities, better manage your emotions, and set boundaries to protect your energy. Quizzes and prompts will guide you through the process.

We've got a lot to cover, so let's get started.

An empath overwhelmed by daily life can develop a fear of others, a disconnect from their body, and a disdain for who they are. In short, they do not feel safe being themselves.

—KRISTEN SCHWARTZ, *The Healed Empath*

What I have realized is that the biggest mistake I made was to underestimate what it means to be an empath. I underestimated myself. I underestimated my needs. I underestimated my sensitivity. I was trying to act like a normal person, as though if I acted like a normal person hard enough, somehow things would be different.

—JENNIFER ELIZABETH MOORE, *Empathic Mastery*

what it means to be an empath

Humans aren't as good as we should be in our capacity to empathize with feelings and thoughts of others... maybe part of our formal education should be training in empathy. Imagine how different the world would be if, in fact, that were reading, writing, arithmetic, and empathy.

—NEIL DEGRASSE TYSON, astrophysicist and author

Chapter 1

WHAT IS AN EMPATH?

Many of us are highly sensitive, acutely aware of our own and other people's feelings, but when you're also an empath, your sensitivity goes deeper. Simply explained, empathy is the act of coming to experience the world as you think or perceive someone else does. It's witnessing someone's struggle and taking on your interpretation of their feelings, as if they were your own. A highly sensitive person feels empathy for someone in distress and may express compassion or sympathy to help alleviate the person's distress. An empath, on the other hand, is capable of *feeling* what the person in distress feels, as if that person's trauma is also happening to them. As an empath, unless you learn to set firm boundaries, you may internalize the feelings others experience so deeply that you may neglect your own needs.

The concept of empathy as a force for good has been so popular in recent years that more than 1,500 books have been published, encouraging people to increasingly notice and respond to what others may be struggling to survive; by doing so, they will—hopefully—become more compassionate, kind, and generous.

While increased compassion for others is absolutely a positive thing, and most of us do need to bolster our ability to be more empathetic, some people are so highly empathic that they quite literally feel other people's feelings. This amount of empathy comes with its own set of baggage, including:

- It can lead to empaths becoming so focused on others (and world events, tragedies, mass murders, crime, their neighbor's problems, etc.) that they stop doing what they need to do for themselves. True empaths may struggle to focus on their own lives, their feelings, even their life goals.

- Empaths can also experience "empath fatigue" or even go into "hyper-empath" mode, which leads to all kinds of physical and emotional problems that can detract from their ability to enjoy their lives. (We'll describe both in Chapter 2.)

- True empaths may assume they know what others are thinking or feeling and why they're doing things the way they are; but they can be wrong, which can negatively affect relationships.

Being a highly sensitive person or an empath is a good thing; it's an admirable way to be, as long as you create parameters, ways to use what's essentially your superpower without sacrificing your own well-being. This book is designed to help empaths—and highly sensitive people—understand themselves better, heal whatever wounds have been created, prioritize self-care, learn to set boundaries, and better manage their emotions.

Where would humanity be without empathy? Our lives would be disconnected, our societies would fall apart.

—FRANS DE WAAL, *The Age of Empathy*

EMPATHS ARE HIGHLY SENSITIVE

Since you've picked up this book, you identify as or consider yourself to be an empath. Like other empaths, you are more likely to be highly sensitive to stimuli like loud noises, jumbled cacophonies, other people's raging emotions, or violent scenarios. You can become so affected by others' moods that overstimulation can cause nervous exhaustion. Empaths tend to be hyper-aware of others' emotional states (and all the subtle nuances associated with them) and often deeply empathize with others. This isn't necessarily a bad thing—if it's moderated and does not detract from your personal welfare.

While highly sensitive people become adept at picking up signals that clue them in to how other people feel, those who are also empaths, on the other hand, don't need visual or auditory clues to know how someone is feeling. If you're an empath, you have the *distinct and unusual* ability to sense and *feel* others' emotions, as if it were *your own* pain.

You're not imagining it. Studies have shown that empath brains tend to have more mirror neurons—neurons that unconsciously respond to others and allow us to connect on a deeper level. Their mirror neurons communicate the information and lead empaths to feel whatever the other person feels, *as if it's also happening to them*. Their empathy exceeds what's normal for highly sensitive people and can cause trauma that requires healing. And that's what we'll be doing in this book.

EMPATH QUIZ

If you're wondering whether you're just a burned-out highly sensitive person, or an empath in need of healing, the following quiz will help you know for certain. Answer "yes" or "no" to each question. If it's mostly true or more often true, answer "yes."

YES	NO	
☐	☐	Do strangers often latch onto you and quickly overshare their life with you?
☐	☐	Do you regularly need a lot of alone time to recharge?
☐	☐	Does violent content on the news or in movies rattle you to the point of discomfort?
☐	☐	Have you often been told you are far more sensitive than most others?
☐	☐	Have you often been chastised for what others consider "overly emotional" reactions?
☐	☐	Do you hesitate to reveal your true self, fearing you'll be judged and rejected?
☐	☐	Do you have difficulty creating and sustaining interpersonal boundaries?
☐	☐	Were you so traumatized early in life that you are hypervigilant and easily triggered?
☐	☐	Do you feel so overwhelmed in crowds or at significant events that you severely limit your social life?
☐	☐	Are you guided by, highly sensitive to, or aware that you have a finely tuned intuition?
☐	☐	Do you often sense what someone is thinking or feeling before they speak?
☐	☐	If someone you care about is experiencing strong emotions, does it make you feel those same emotions?
☐	☐	Is it painful to be around someone who is emotionally or physically distressed?
☐	☐	Does your nervous system often feel overwhelmed, and are you often anxious?
☐	☐	Is getting sufficient, restorative sleep more essential to you than most?
☐	☐	Do you often prioritize others' wellness over your own?

If you answered more than ten questions with a "yes" response, you are likely an empath in need of healing.

When you're an empath, you have the ability to observe another person to the point that you know what they're thinking and/or sense their feelings; you might also *feel* their feelings (in a muted but still impactful and often distracting way). The other person's emotion can overpower your own emotion. Empaths are highly sensitive and almost reflexively responsive to emotional clues such as facial expressions, word choices, body language, and actions such as crying, smiling, shrinking back, shaking, and so on. But it's not just a reflex; it's a skill that can be nurtured, supported, consciously directed, and wisely used to your own and other's advantage. These are all topics we'll cover in this book.

AIM FOR COMPASSION

If someone was stuck in a quagmire:

Sympathy would be: sitting on the side, feeling sorry for them.

Empathy would be: getting into the quagmire with them and trying to find a way out for both of you.

Compassion would be: keeping your own feet on solid ground and staying in a state of love while you reach out a hand or branch to help them to get out.

— ODILLE REMMERT, author

Empathy is a constant awareness of the fact that your concerns are not everyone's concerns and that your needs are not everyone's needs.

—ROMAN KRZNARIC, *Empathy*

THREE TYPES OF EMPATHS

Not all empaths are the same. Although you may experience various levels of empathy, you likely tend toward one of the following three types:

Cognitive: Also known as social intelligence, mind reading, or mentalizing. You use critical thinking to know and understand what someone else is *thinking*, to understand their perspective. You also understand their feelings and can sympathize by putting yourself in their shoes.

Emotional: What someone else is feeling may affect your emotional state. You not only know what someone is feeling, you may take on their feelings, or *feel what they feel*. You may also feel your own pain in response to their distress and feel compassion for them. You are capable of sharing someone else's emotional experience.

Intuitive: You experience life with *extraordinary perceptions* and may have psychic ability that can manifest as a sense of knowing, openness to telepathy, and ability to receive messages in dreams.

Emotional empaths are the ones most likely to get too caught up in other people's trauma, neglect their own needs, and eventually burn out. This book is being offered primarily as a guide for emotional empaths to heal any wounds caused by being too empathetic, learn how to protect their own energy, and better manage how and when they employ empathy.

IDEAL EMPATHY

The least problematic form of empathy is compassionate empathy, which means you not only understand a person's situation but ensure they receive what is morally and ethically fair. It's highly desirable, as you not only have the ability to empathize with what someone else is feeling or experiencing but you are not so emotional that you can't step in to help them change it. It leads to prosocial behaviors, such as volunteering to help a charitable organization. Compassionate empathy is considered healthy, and those with it are not as likely to experience *hyper-empathy* or suffer burnout.

Are you primarily a cognitive, emotional, or intuitive empath?

_____

_____

_____

_____

_____

_____

_____

_____

How does your empathy typically manifest?

_____

_____

_____

_____

_____

_____

_____

_____

What problems, if any, is it currently causing?

_____

_____

_____

_____

_____

_____

_____

_____

_____

_____

_____

_____

_____

_____

_____

_____

_____

If you're primarily an emotional empath, who answered mostly "yes" to many of the quiz questions on page 15, you likely need both support and a pathway to healing. Let's start by discussing where empaths get into trouble.

Learning to stand in somebody else's shoes, to see through their eyes, that's how peace begins. And it's up to you to make that happen. Empathy is a quality of character that can change the world.

—BARACK OBAMA,
44th president of the United States

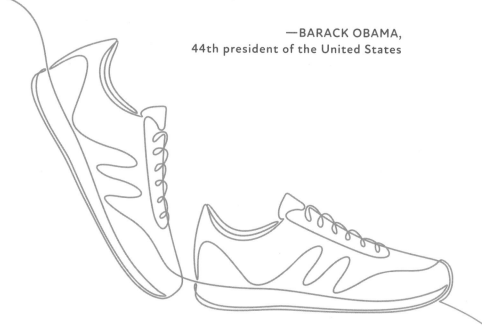

Chapter 2

WHERE EMPATHS GET INTO TROUBLE

Being an empath has many positives. It typically means that you are more kind, generous, and thoughtful than most people. Your super sensitivity makes you a good listener, someone trusted friends can turn to during challenging times, and we all know how valuable that can be. It can also make you more responsive and thereby spur others to pay more attention to what matters. Empaths have a broader ability to feel compassion for others, which leads you to willfully extend kindness.

Also, when you feel supercharged and share your positivity, it can inspire others to open their hearts and feel freer to express themselves. Your upbeat, forward-thinking energy can boost creative energy in the room. It can even help at work, where social skills make it easier to work in teams and support your coworkers. Empaths can be highly intuitive and sense when someone is being insincere, which helps you avoid disastrous relationships.

Some of the many benefits of being an empath are:

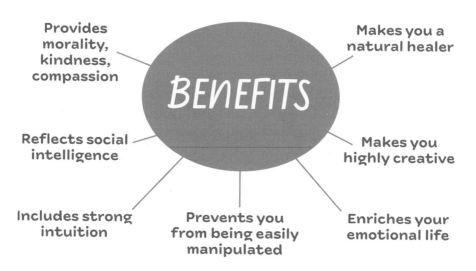

Provides morality, kindness, compassion

Makes you a natural healer

BENEFITS

Reflects social intelligence

Makes you highly creative

Includes strong intuition

Prevents you from being easily manipulated

Enriches your emotional life

Which of the previous positives do you happily experience?

_____

_____

_____

_____

_____

_____

_____

_____

_____

Which ones are you using to your advantage?

_____

_____

_____

_____

_____

_____

_____

_____

Which benefits do you need to recognize or cultivate more often?

1. _____

_____

2. _____

_____

3. _____

_____

4. _____

_____

5. _____

_____

Can you identify even more positives of being an empath?

_____

_____

_____

_____

_____

_____

_____

_____

Write about a time when you felt lucky to be an empath. What happened? How did your gift manifest?

_____

_____

_____

_____

_____

_____

_____

_____

Make a list of occasions when your empathic qualities truly worked to your advantage and briefly state why.

_____

_____

_____

_____

_____

_____

_____

_____

WHERE EMPATHS GO WRONG

So, yes, being an empath is a gift, something you should value about yourself and make the most of in your life. Empaths are fabulously caring, creative, and uplifting humans, with much to contribute and lots of love to share. When used properly, it is a superpower.

Unfortunately, empaths are also susceptible to feeling *too* deeply, being *too* tuned in to others, being *too* giving. When an empath consistently focuses more on the people around them and not enough on themselves, things can start to go haywire. You can reach a point where you're in "hyper-empath" mode, so tuned in to those around you that you lose sight of *your* needs and fail to honor *your* boundaries or provide the kind of self-care needed to restore *your* energy.

EMPATH CONTINUUM

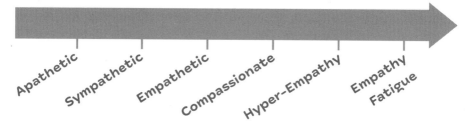

Apathetic   Sympathetic   Empathetic   Compassionate   Hyper-Empathy   Empathy Fatigue

Being *too* sensitive and *too* focused on what others are feeling and being "on" all the time becomes exhausting, increasing your stress levels. If it goes on too long, it can lead to empath fatigue and other problems, including:

Need to please or take care of others

Extreme sensitivity

Poor communication

Codependency

Shortsightedness

Shame

DRAWBACKS

Hiding what you feel

Lack of boundaries

Anxiety

Low self-esteem (you assume you're the cause of other people's bad feelings)

Losing sight of your own needs

Difficulty regulating emotions

Strained relationships

Which of the previous drawbacks are bogging you down?

_____

_____

_____

_____

_____

_____

_____

_____

What can you do to address them?

_____

_____

_____

_____

_____

_____

_____

_____

_____

Write about a time when you offered empathy to someone, which usually made you feel good about yourself, but you ended up feeling particularly drained, stressed, or overwhelmed. What caused it to flip from a positive to a negative?

_____

_____

_____

_____

_____

_____

THE DARK SIDE OF BEING AN EMPATH

Psychopaths are often cognitive empaths (see page 18) who can discern what others are thinking, feeling, or needing and then intentionally use that information as a weapon to cruelly exploit them. Psychopaths typically lack emotional empathy. Because narcissists thrive on someone worshipping them, they are often attracted to highly compassionate and understanding empaths who more easily fall sway to codependent relationships.

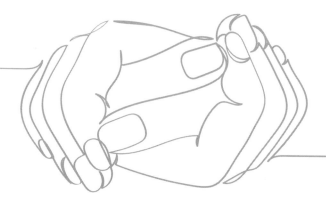

For there is nothing heavier
than compassion. Not even
one's own pain weighs so
heavy as the pain one feels
with someone, for someone,
a pain intensified by the
imagination and prolonged by
a hundred echoes.

—MILAN KUNDERA, *The Unbearable Lightness of Being*

ARE YOU STUCK IN HYPER-EMPATH MODE?

As we've seen, being a highly sensitive empath has many positives. Yet, because you are so kind, without proper management and conscious mitigation, you are more susceptible to reaching *hyper*-empath mode: being constantly available to help others, while concurrently neglecting yourself. You can become so empathic toward others' emotions and feelings that you are not tending to your own emotional needs, safeguarding your physical and mental health, or doing anything to nurture yourself. When you're caught up in hyper-empathy, you may feel generous, caring, and noble, but if you don't dial it back, you are putting yourself on the path to burnout or emotional breakdown.

WHY RELATIONSHIPS CAN BE STRAINED

Empathy allows us to bond with other people. However, empaths in "hyper mode" tend to be so sensitive to what someone else is feeling that they put the other person's emotions first and lose sight of what they themselves need and feel, even who they are. The closeness of an intimate relationship may leave them feeling overwhelmed by their beloved's emotions.

In *The Empath's Survival Guide*, Judith Orloff, MD, explains that all humans have a "specialized group of brain cells that are responsible for compassion," but when one is in *hyper*-empath mode, those cells become overstimulated and "hyper-responsive." To help you know whether your cells are currently hyper-responsive, answer "yes" or "no" to the following questions. If it's mostly true, choose "yes."

YES   NO

☐   ☐   Have you recently been accused of being too emotional or overly sensitive?

☐   ☐   When a friend is distraught, do you feel so equally distraught that it leaves you also feeling incapacitated?

☐   ☐   Have you been so attentive to others that you feel resentful?

☐   ☐   Are your feelings being so easily hurt that you've been withdrawing?

☐   ☐   Have you been feeling more emotionally drained than usual?

☐   ☐   Is being in crowds sapping so much energy you need a lot of time alone to revive?

☐   ☐   Have noises, smells, or excessive talk been fraying your emotions?

☐   ☐   Have you been driving your own car places so you can make a quick exit?

☐   ☐   Have you been overeating, overdrinking, or using drugs to cope with emotional stress?

☐   ☐   Have you been so afraid of becoming engulfed by intimate relationships that you've been avoiding intimacy for years?

☐   ☐   Have you been feeling so drained after social gatherings that you consistently avoid them?

☐   ☐   Are you having difficulty saying "no," even when the ask is too much?

☐   ☐   Are you consistently putting others' needs first, and yours last?

☐   ☐   Have you been so caught up in feeling sorry for others that you tolerate their unkind behavior?

☐   ☐   Do your emotions feel so overwhelming you have difficulty maintaining preferred standards in your daily life?

If you answered "yes" to as few as three of the questions, it may indicate that you are dealing with hyper-empathy.

Did any of the quiz questions surprise you? Or did you identify something you consistently do, without realizing it was harming you?

_____

_____

_____

_____

_____

_____

_____

_____

Circle the symptoms that require immediate attention, and then write down any that may not be on the list.

_____

_____

_____

_____

_____

_____

_____

_____

INEFFECTIVE COPING METHODS

If you've been in hyper-empath mode for a long time, you may have fallen sway to the following negative coping methods:

- Choosing withdrawal or isolation
- Avoiding people and situations
- Employing distraction
- Blaming others and yourself
- Succumbing to addiction

If you've been coping ineffectively, take heart. We'll discuss many approaches to cope in ways that restore and rejuvenate rather than deplete you.

Peace of mind for five minutes, that's what I crave.

—ALANIS MORISSETTE, singer and songwriter

HOW TO CALM HYPER-EMPATHY IN THE MOMENT

Luckily, there are some tactics you can employ to reduce hyper-empathy and better control your emotions. In an article for *Psychology Today*, psychologist Marcia Reynolds, PsyD, recommends four simple steps for immediate relief:

1. Relax: If possible, sit down somewhere quiet. Breathe slowly in and out, focusing solely on your breath, until you feel calm. Notice any tension being held in your body and release it. Offer yourself compassion.

2. Detach from the emotion: Stop mentally obsessing about whatever situation caused the strong emotions. Purposefully release any negative thoughts. Emotions should flow through you, not consume you.

3. Center your awareness: Drop your awareness to the center of your body, just below your navel. Place a hand on your belly, then breathe slowly in and out, feeling each breath, until your mind clears and emotions dissipate.

4. Focus on alternatives: Create one or two keywords to represent how you *want* to feel. Then use your superior curiosity to come up with ways to create the desired feelings.

Empathic overarousal often happens to nurses on cancer wards or humanitarian aid workers. They [are forced to] become good at switching [their empathy] off and getting on with their jobs.

—ROMAN KRZNARIC, *Empathy*

ARE YOU EXPERIENCING EMPATHY FATIGUE?

In an article published on the Cleveland Clinic's *Health Essentials* blog, Susan Albers, PsyD, defines empathy fatigue as emotional and physical exhaustion that stems from caring for people day after day after day. For empaths, repeated exposure to stressful or traumatic events that others are experiencing can cause *you* to experience emotional and physical symptoms. Empathy fatigue is "your body's way of telling you to pay attention and to take a step back to care for yourself," Dr. Albers writes.

Empathy fatigue is a defense mechanism.

—SUSAN ALBERS, PsyD

Empathy fatigue happens when caring for others depletes your internal resources to care for yourself. To find out if you're experiencing empathy fatigue, answer "yes" or "no" to the questions in the following quiz. If it's mostly true, choose "yes." There's not a magic number of "yes" answers to indicate that you are or are not experiencing empathy fatigue; rather, this quiz will shed light on symptoms that you need to examine.

YES	NO	
☐	☐	Are you feeling weighed down by relationships?
☐	☐	Are you having trouble concentrating, being productive, or completing simple tasks?
☐	☐	Do you strongly prefer being alone?
☐	☐	Have you been choosing isolation more often than socializing?
☐	☐	Do you cut conversations short?
☐	☐	Do you feel overwhelmed by other people's problems?
☐	☐	Are you often tense or easily agitated?
☐	☐	Are you experiencing headaches, nausea, or an upset stomach?
☐	☐	Does noise startle and annoy you?
☐	☐	Does being around too many people stress you out?
☐	☐	Does making small talk try your patience?
☐	☐	Are you more irritable, annoyed, or short tempered than usual?
☐	☐	Are you feeling cynical about yourself and others?
☐	☐	Are you obsessing about other people's suffering?
☐	☐	Does feeling overwhelmed leave you feeling powerless or hopeless?
☐	☐	Have you been feeling disconnected or numb?
☐	☐	Do you often feel tired, sad, or depressed?
☐	☐	Are you neglecting your own emotional needs?
☐	☐	Are you oversharing your problems?
☐	☐	Are you self-medicating with food, alcohol, or drugs?

YES NO

☐ ☐ Are you worrying so much it's causing distress?

☐ ☐ Are you having difficulty getting restorative sleep?

How many of the previous symptoms are you experiencing?

_____

_____

_____

_____

_____

_____

Circle any symptoms you are experiencing that are most concerning. Which three need immediate attention?

1. _____

_____

_____

2. _____

_____

_____

3. _____

_____

_____

What could you do to provide relief for those things that need immediate attention?

1. _____

_____

_____

_____

_____

_____

2. _____

_____

_____

_____

_____

_____

3. _____

_____

_____

_____

_____

_____

TRY THE ABC APPROACH

If you are experiencing empathy fatigue, Dr. Albers suggests beginning with what she calls an "ABC approach":

A = **Awareness.** Acknowledge how you've been feeling by taking a moment to name and feel it, noticing how it feels in your body and mind. Realize that feelings are transitory, then release them, and offer yourself compassion.

B = **Balance.** Make sure you are balancing any worrisome activities (doomscrolling, obsessing, being too focused on others) with self-care. Focus on activities that nurture your emotional health, such as eating well, exercising, meditating, or doing something that replenishes your energy reserves.

C = **Connection.** Connect with people who love and support you. Reach out for the extra emotional or moral support *you* need.

Note that this book will offer you many ways to heal and better modulate your sensitivity.

LEARN TO MANAGE EMPATHY FATIGUE

It's important to remember that you have a responsibility to monitor and regulate how much or how little you empathize. Here are three methods you can use to manage empathy fatigue:

1. Love your intuition but know when to turn it off or override it. When you feel overwhelmed, you can choose not to pay attention and trust others to manage their emotions without your help. You can remind yourself that you need to focus on you.

2. Create a burnout metaphor. Describe how it viscerally feels when you are burned out:

> "I feel like everyone has a cord attached to my heart and is literally pulling on me."
>
> "I feel stranded in a dark tunnel with blinders on and weights attached to my legs."
>
> "I feel like I've been clinging to a deflating life raft, in freezing waters for days."

3. Visualize rescuing yourself. Use your vivid imagination to create and execute a rescue plan.

What is your current burnout metaphor?

_____

_____

_____

_____

_____

_____

How can you rescue yourself from hyper-empathy or empathy burnout? Write your rescue plan.

_____

_____

_____

_____

_____

_____

_____

_____

_____

_____

_____

_____

_____

_____

_____

_____

_____

_____

Now that we've discussed the harmful drawbacks associated with being an empath, particularly those associated with hyper-empathy and empath fatigue, we'll move on to the healing strategies and later, to methods for more properly managing your emotional health.

A portion of empaths I've treated have experienced early trauma, such as emotional or physical abuse, or were raised by alcoholic, depressed, or narcissistic parents. This could potentially wear down the usual healthy defenses that a child with nurturing parents develops. As a result of their upbringing, these [highly sensitive] children typically don't feel 'seen' by their families, and they also feel invisible in the greater world that doesn't value sensitivity.

—JUDITH ORLOFF, MD, *The Empath's Survival Guide*

PART II

healing strategies

The sad thing that many of us empaths don't realize is that often our desire to heal others is a disguised cry for help for our own healing. Because many of us weren't taught how to value or nurture ourselves at a young age, we tend to unconsciously seek out our own healing in the healing of others.

—ALETHEIA LUNA AND MATEO SOL,
Awakened Empath

Chapter 3

IDENTIFY YOUR INITIAL TRAUMA

Often, our high sensitivity has its genesis in childhood trauma; whatever happened may have seemed "normal" at the time yet still caused an emotional earthquake. Trauma comes in many forms; it needn't have been a catastrophic event. It could result from ongoing neglect, verbal abuse, or a parent with addiction issues. Those who develop high sensitivity and become overly empathic may have experienced one or more of the following traumas:

- You had a hypersensitive parent or caregiver who may have often felt overwhelmed or suffered from anxiety.

- You had a parent or caregiver who often behaved erratically or unpredictably.

- You had a parent or caregiver who was often angry and controlling.

- You had a parent or caregiver who was often absent or aloof and emotionally unavailable.

- Your family never established emotional boundaries; no one took accountability for his/her own emotions, so you accepted them as yours.

- An adult or caregiver took advantage of your sensitivity by relying too heavily on you.

- Your life often felt overwhelming and overstimulating, which caused you to feel anxious or retreat.

- Someone in your family died from a devastating illness or accident.

- You were severely ill or injured and required a long recovery.

- One of your family members succumbed to alcoholism, workaholism, or drug addiction.

- Someone in your childhood environment abused you emotionally, verbally, physically, or sexually.

WERE YOU TRAUMATIZED?

It's often hard for children to know they're experiencing trauma, especially if it's long-term and seems "normal."

Some symptoms a child is experiencing sensitivity-induced trauma include:

- Disturbed sleep, feels anxious or depressed

- Nervousness, alertness, or hypervigilance

- A need to deny or numb feelings, withdrawal

- Difficulty showing or accepting affection

- Avoidance of certain people, places, or things

- Difficulty focusing or conveying feelings

The aftereffects of trauma that contributed to becoming overly empathic and show up in adulthood include:

- Extreme sensitivity

- Fear of abandonment

- A compulsion to please others

- Feeling hurt, vulnerable, or ashamed

- Feeling afraid, avoidance as a strategy

- Taking on too much responsibility

Using the list on page 50 as a guideline, write down any and all primary traumas you experienced. Yours may or may not be on the list, but it's highly likely something (either traumatic or ongoing) contributed to you becoming an empath. List any and all traumas below.

1. _____

_____

2. _____

_____

3. _____

_____

4. _____

_____

5. _____

_____

6. _____

_____

7. _____

_____

Which ones have caused you the most pain?

_____

_____

_____

_____

_____

_____

_____

_____

_____

How have they specifically affected you?

_____

_____

_____

_____

_____

_____

_____

_____

_____

You may not control all the events that happen to you, but you can decide not to be reduced by them.

—MAYA ANGELOU, poet and civil rights activist

DETERMINE HOW YOUR TRAUMAS AFFECTED WHO YOU BECAME

Once you have recognized that what happened *truly did happen*, it's helpful to see that how you coped as a child has led to your current hypersensitivity, as well as any problems relating to others that you're experiencing as an adult. There are many ways highly sensitive children respond or adapt, including the below list. To get a better handle on how trauma may have affected you as a child, answer "yes" or "no" to the following questions; if it's mostly true, choose "yes."

YES	NO	
☐	☐	Did you do your best to juggle everyone's feelings?
☐	☐	Did you literally caretake for one or both parents?
☐	☐	Were you angry that your parents relied on you for emotional support?
☐	☐	Did you consistently offer more love than you received?
☐	☐	Did anyone shame you for your high sensitivity?
☐	☐	Did you feel you had to suppress or deny your feelings?
☐	☐	Did you withdraw or hide your true self?
☐	☐	When you felt responsible, did you punish yourself?
☐	☐	Did you feel exceptionally burdened, overwhelmed, or frightened?
☐	☐	Did you develop anxiety or depression?

Referring to your earlier list of traumas (page 52), go through each and spend time contemplating, from your adult perspective, how each trauma affected your emotional development and how you learned to adapt.

1. _____

_____

2. _____

_____

3. _____

_____

4. _____

_____

5. _____

_____

6. _____

_____

7. _____

_____

Do you see any patterns? If so, what are they?

The struggle of my life
created empathy—I could
relate to pain, being
abandoned, having people
not love me.

—OPRAH WINFREY,
television producer and author

Can you forgive yourself for doing whatever you could to cope, even if it proved hurtful? What would you say to the highly sensitive child you were?

_____

_____

_____

_____

_____

_____

_____

_____

Do you see healthier ways to respond now? What would that look like?

_____

_____

_____

_____

_____

_____

_____

_____

_____

_____

PATHWAYS TO HEALING

Now that you have identified traumas that likely contributed to being in hyper-empath mode, let's discuss methods you can use to heal the initial trauma and free yourself to move on.

We cannot hate ourselves into being better versions of ourselves. It's impossible. Love, patience, and understanding have to be at the center of our healing.

—ALEXANDRA ELLE, *How We Heal*

NURTURE YOUR INNER CHILD

Often, when strong emotions arise, the distress they cause stems from something similar (and emotionally traumatic) that happened to you in childhood. For example, if you see a parent verbally berating a child and your heart starts to pound, it's likely your parent was verbally abusive at times and when it happened, you felt powerless to protest. If something is consistently causing you distress, take five minutes to remember, and mentally recreate, a time in childhood when something similar happened and you felt this same emotion, or something similar.

What was the trauma?

_____

_____

_____

_____

_____

_____

_____

_____

_____

_____

_____

_____

How did you respond, short-term and long-term?

_____

_____

_____

_____

_____

_____

_____

_____

How is the initial trauma and your response to it still affecting you?

_____

_____

_____

_____

_____

_____

_____

_____

_____

_____

As you sit quietly, imagine that traumatized child sitting across from you. Spend a few minutes closely observing how this child feels. Ask the child to vocalize their thoughts and fears. What would you say to that child to reassure them that the emotions they're experiencing are understandable and that they have the resources to manage whatever comes?

_____

_____

_____

_____

_____

_____

_____

_____

_____

_____

_____

_____

Do this often enough and it will help you heal past trauma and help you remember that you have the ability to process and redirect whatever emotions have surfaced.

List the five most distressing events or situations in your childhood that left you feeling traumatized. These may differ from those traumas you wrote about on page 52.

1. _____

2. _____

3. _____

4. _____

5. _____

In each case, how would you reassure your inner child that you are now able to cope with similar events or situations? What would you now advise your inner child to do?

1. _____

_____

2. _____

_____

3. _____

_____

4. _____

_____

5. _____

_____

I was born a little broken,
with an extra dose of
sensitivity.

—GLENNON DOYLE, author of
Untamed and *Love Warrior*

WRITE IT OUT

One of the best ways to heal past trauma is to write about what happened, how everyone responded, how it made you feel, how you learned to cope with similar situations, and how it has continued to impact you. Even though it may feel painful, write about your most significant traumas with as much detail as possible, particularly how you felt and reacted in those moments, and in the months and years that followed.

_____

_____

_____

_____

_____

_____

_____

_____

_____

_____

_____

_____

_____

_____

_____

_____

_____

FORGIVE YOURSELF

Traumatized children often blame themselves for both the trauma *and* how they adapted. Highly sensitive children often punish themselves for how they reacted to damaging circumstances. You may consciously or unconsciously judge yourself for developing the habits that helped you cope the way you did. As an adult, before you move forward, it's important to forgive yourself for the past.

What do you want to forgive your younger self for doing? Can you see now that you did the best you could at the time?

_____

_____

_____

_____

_____

_____

_____

_____

_____

_____

_____

_____

_____

Forgiveness is not a gift for another person. At its core, it has nothing to do with anyone but you. Forgiveness is something you do for yourself, so that the past no longer has a hold on you.

—BARB SCHMIDT,
Cofounder of Peaceful Mind Peaceful Life

DO A FORGIVENESS MEDITATION

Spend five minutes meditating, during which time you offer yourself forgiveness for any and all trauma-generated adaptations you made in your life. You can find a wealth of meditation guidance online, but it can be something as simple as, "I forgive myself for cowering / believing / punishing myself / hiding my sensitivity after my parent scolded me for being "'too sensitive.'" Hold each trauma adaptation in your mind, then purposefully release them, as if they were birds you release to the sky. Repeat the meditation until you feel purged of any guilt or shame.

How did you feel after this meditation?

_____

_____

_____

_____

_____

_____

_____

_____

_____

_____

_____

_____

_____

Don't allow your trauma to become your identity. Your past is what you experienced and not your destination. You are not the worst thing that ever happened to you. You are not the worst thing you ever did. You are not the meanest thing you ever said to someone.

—JOHN DELONY, PhD, *Redefining Anxiety*

OFFER GRACE TO YOURSELF

Vigilance is no longer needed and being (or doing) whatever you thought you had to be (or do) no longer needs to affect your identity, or what you do going forward. You can release the past trauma and all the dysfunctional behavior that came with it. As you do so, remember to forgive yourself for coping the way you learned to do. You did the best you could at the time, and now you are *choosing* a new way of being.

Write a letter to yourself, in which you express both understanding and forgiveness. Reassure your inner child that how he/she adapted to their environment was all they knew to do at the time and was not their fault. Promise this wounded child that you now know better and will do better.

_____

_____

_____

_____

_____

_____

_____

_____

_____

_____

_____

_____

_____

Healing is a never-ending
journey. Even when I think
I've moved past something,
life throws a curveball my
way that takes me right
back to a place of self-doubt
and negative self-talk.

—ALEXANDRA ELLE, *How We Heal*

Chapter 4

IDENTIFY YOUR VULNERABILITIES

Now that you've rescued your inner child and forgiven yourself for how you adapted to trauma, let's discuss what makes you feel vulnerable and reactive in the present. Once you identify what causes current traumas, you'll be able to lessen their impact and modify your response, both of which will help you balance being an empath with providing the self-care you so desperately need.

IDENTIFY YOUR TRIGGERS

Any dysfunctional coping method—always being available, taking on other people's emotions, being hyper-vigilant, overreacting, withdrawing—is so ingrained that it will take time to make your new coping methods a habit. Learning to identify what sends you spiraling backwards will help you know when it's essential to practice new coping methods. We all have situations that *trigger* our past trauma and how we learned to cope with it.

According to Sherianna Boyle, author of *Energy in Action*, being triggered is like striking an old wound. Most of us have physical or emotional responses that let us know we've been triggered, such as:

- You feel emotionally charged.

- You don't feel in control of your reactions.

- You feel tightness in your chest, face, or jaw.

- You succumb to ruminating thoughts or obsessions.

- You fall sway to your usual chronic overthinking.

- You flip-flop or suddenly change your mind.

- You are eager and willing to do anything to avoid the feelings generated.

- You experience quick, impulsive, panicked, or urgent thoughts and behaviors, even though there is no imminent threat or clear problem.

Make a list of situations or people who most often trigger you, why, and how you know you've been triggered.

1. _____

_____

2. _____

_____

3. _____

_____

4. _____

_____

5. _____

_____

Once you've identified your triggers, use this knowledge to recognize them *when* they occur and then pause until you feel able to *choose* a new way to respond.

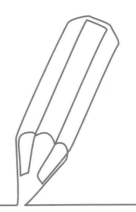

KNOW YOUR HAPPINESS TRIGGERS

Just as you have triggers that can send you into a negative spiral, you can have things that trigger happiness. Such things could include:

- A long hug from a loved one

- Cooking your favorite meal

- Doing a craft you love

- Creating music or art

- Meditating

- Singing

- Dancing to a song that pumps you up

- Performing an act of kindness (buy a stranger a cup of coffee, clean out your closet and donate clothing and shoes, deliver a homemade cake to a neighbor) Enjoying your favorite beverage (in your favorite place)

- Seeing, smelling, or touching someone or something you love (a healing crystal or stone, the special necklace your mother gave you, your collection of angel figurines)

When you know your happiness triggers, you can actively use them to boost your mood; make sure to savor the moment!

What specific activities make you happy?

_____

_____

_____

_____

_____

_____

_____

_____

Which people make you feel loved and supported or bring you the greatest joy?

_____

_____

_____

_____

_____

_____

_____

_____

_____

What do you love doing (and rarely make time for)?

What movies, art, songs, or foods make you feel happy?

> Leading with integrity and empathy requires vision and a connection to your deepest self.
>
> —KARLA MCLAREN, *The Art of Empathy*

RECOGNIZE YOUR WANTS AND NEEDS

Make a list of what you need and what you want, focusing on emotional needs and wants, not things. Maybe you *need* your partner to offer you their undivided attention for at least fifteen minutes every day and truly listen to what concerns you; maybe you *want* them to ask you out on a date once a month to create happy memories.

Dig deep to figure out what you really want and need from others, or yourself, to feel loved, safe, nurtured, secure, and happy. Notice if you experience any difficulty creating these lists. After all, empaths have learned to care more about others than themselves and have learned to ignore their own wants and needs. This is an exercise you can repeat whenever you feel that you're losing sight of your own wants and needs.

What You Need	What You Want

1. _____   _____
   _____   _____

2. _____   _____
   _____   _____

3. _____   _____
   _____   _____

4. _____   _____
   _____   _____

5. _____   _____
   _____   _____

6. _____   _____
   _____   _____

7. _____   _____
   _____   _____

8. _____   _____
   _____   _____

9. _____   _____
   _____   _____

10. _____   _____
    _____   _____

TRY A WORTHY MEDITATION

If you have trouble identifying your wants and needs, Alexandra Elle, author of *How We Heal*, suggests an "I am worthy" meditation. Use the items below as your "worthy mantras" (or create your own). Then, slow your breathing until you feel relaxed and receptive. Slowly repeat your mantras to yourself, for yourself (it's okay to read a list during meditation).

- I can ask for what I need.

- I can vocalize what I want.

- I am worthy of having my needs met.

- I can show up as my full self.

- I am growing and healing.

After your "worthy" meditation, write about how owning those declarations felt. Did they come easily, did you believe them, or did they make you feel selfish or uncomfortable?

_____

_____

_____

_____

_____

_____

_____

_____

_____

_____

_____

_____

_____

_____

Repeat this exercise until your worthy mantras become ingrained. You can also write them out and tape them somewhere you'll see them often. Or record them on your phone so you can listen to them when needed.

Between stimulus and response, there is a space. In that space lies our freedom and power to choose our response. In our response lies our growth and freedom.

—VIKTOR E. FRANKL, *Man's Search for Meaning*

FLIP NEGATIVE THOUGHTS TO POSITIVE ONES

One way to let go of nonproductive coping mechanisms is to *choose* how you think. It can be as simple as noticing when negative thoughts bog you down, and then quickly replacing those negative thoughts with positive thoughts.

According to Charlene Rymsha, author of *Burn Bright,* it's as simple as doing the following:

1. When you recognize a negative thought or negative pattern of thinking, immediately stop yourself from accepting, saying, or repeating it.

2. Label it as a negative or unhelpful thought or pattern.

3. Embrace the process by saying, "From now on I choose only helpful thoughts and patterns of thinking that support my well-being."

4. Create a positive, helpful statement to replace the old thought or pattern of thinking.

Example: You're at dinner with a close friend who berates you for being "too sensitive," and you respond by shrinking into your seat and agreeing with her. Instead of your usual pattern, stop. Tell yourself: "This is not a helpful thought or pattern." Say (aloud or silently): "From now on I choose only helpful thoughts and patterns of thinking that support my well-being." Then, say aloud to your friend: "It's true that I feel things deeply, but I see this as a huge positive, as long as I am learning new ways to respond and no longer take on other people's feelings."

List at least three negative thoughts or patterns of thinking that consistently cause you problems.

1. _____

_____

_____

2. _____

_____

_____

3. _____

_____

_____

Stop, recognize the negative pattern, reinforce your new way of thinking, and then restate what was said to make it what is *true*.

1. _____

_____

_____

2. _____

_____

_____

3. _____

_____

_____

When you're anxious or afraid, what negative thoughts replay in your head?

1. _____

_____

_____

2. _____

_____

_____

3. _____

_____

_____

State that these thoughts are not helpful, then reframe them into positive statements.

1. _____

_____

_____

2. _____

_____

_____

3. _____

_____

_____

TAKE RESPONSIBILITY FOR YOUR ACTIONS

Now that you've identified the way(s) you adapted to your primary traumas, it's important to realize that you now have full responsibility for how you respond. As an awakened adult empath, *it's up to you* to remove yourself from unhealthy situations and limit exposure to people who don't honor or support your emotional well-being.

The way the world operates can crush a lot of our spirits. We think we have to keep showing up in certain environments, and we have to keep going back to bury ourselves and soldier on. A part of my healing is remembering that I have agency and freedom to walk out of places that are insulting my soul.

—GLENNON DOYLE, author of
Untamed and *Love Warrior*

List five situations or people that you will choose to better manage or avoid, and why it's necessary for you to walk away.

1. _____

_____

_____

_____

2. _____

_____

_____

_____

3. _____

_____

_____

_____

4. _____

_____

_____

_____

5. _____

_____

_____

_____

Visualize a person who consistently makes you uncomfortable. Imagine a conversation in which you ask the person to change their behavior toward you and what you would say if they refused. What would you say? What would you do?

_____

_____

_____

_____

_____

_____

_____

_____

_____

_____

_____

_____

_____

_____

_____

_____

_____

I wanted to be more intentional about the health of my relationships. You can just be a relationship collector and have a lot of stuff going on, or you can have some quality relationships. I switched from having a quantity of relationships to having higher-quality ones.

—NEDRA GLOVER TAWWAB,
Set Boundaries, Find Peace

CHOOSE HEALTHY RELATIONSHIPS

The more you heal, the easier it is to choose friendships that support your growth and weed out those that don't.

List the five most supportive people in your life and how they support you.

1. _____

_____

_____

2. _____

_____

_____

3. _____

_____

_____

4. _____

_____

_____

5. _____

_____

_____

List five people who consistently misunderstand, take advantage of, or disrespect you and how this makes you feel.

1. _____

_____

2. _____

_____

3. _____

_____

4. _____

_____

5. _____

_____

Because it's impossible to avoid some people (e.g., family, coworkers), brainstorm ways you can better cope when you're around them.

_____

_____

_____

_____

_____

Awareness of when you feel safe and can let down your guard versus when you need to stay alert and maintain your boundaries will help you choose healthy relationships.

FOCUS ON YOUR STRENGTHS

According to Ryan M. Niemiec and Robert E. McGrath, authors of *The Power of Character Strengths*, people who focus on their character strengths, as opposed to what's wrong in their lives or what they perceive as their own weaknesses, tend to be happier. The idea of cultivating your character strengths derives from positive psychology, which centers on promoting well-being. It's as simple as moving from focusing on *what's wrong in your life* to *what's* **strong** *in your life.*

No leader can ever be great if she or he does not have a profound sense of empathy.

—MICHAEL BESCHLOSS,
presidential historian

Make a list of your strengths, what's working for you, or what you admire about yourself. Spend time contemplating this, and after you complete the list, make sure you review it often and purposefully focus more on *what's strong* than on what's wrong (about your life). It might be hard for you to come up with ten strengths but stick with the process until you do.

1. _____

2. _____

3. _____

4. _____

5. _____

6. _____

7. _____

8. _____

9. _____

10. _____

I had always been a sensitive person with tons of little cracks and as strong and self-reliant as I could act, it took very little for someone to enter those cracks and hurt me.

—JACQUELINE SIMON GUNN, *Where You'll Land*

Chapter 5

BOLSTER YOUR EMOTIONAL RESILIENCE

There's a difference between extreme empathy and compassion. Compassion offers kindness compounded by self-control, intelligent choices, a more diffused focus, and an understanding that any help provided should reflect positive, long-term goals. When you are extending kindness, it helps to first decide whether doing so will lead to more suffering and less thriving, or more pain and less happiness for the recipient. This is easier to do when one feels compassion for many, as opposed to the singular intensity that an empath feels for the plight of one person whose immediate, distressful feelings they are feeling.

According to Paul Bloom, author of *Against Empathy*, empathy can be too focused on one person, creating an "identifiable victim," and thereby narrowing your ability to assess whether aiding that one person helps or hurts their own (or society's) long-term social goals. For example, if you offer money but don't encourage someone in ongoing financial distress to find a new source of income, you may be hurting, rather than truly helping, them. It may be more helpful to suppress an empathetic desire to fix a crisis and focus on providing encouragement (compassion) focused on addressing the long-term underlying causes. Compassion more often leads you to offer help that will address ongoing concerns (such as a person's cancer battle), as opposed to empathy, which often leads you to feel their pain so deeply, you focus on defusing the immediate crisis (such as being upset about test results).

Bloom writes that empathy can equate to a spotlight that creates a myopic viewpoint. He notes that it's almost impossible to empathize with more than one or two people at a time, but possible to have compassion for many. *Feeling* what someone else is feeling may cause you to act impetuously on a single issue or feeling, while having *compassion for* how someone is feeling may encourage you to think broader.

True empaths can have even more difficulty separating incoming emotions from what is truly warranted. The good news is that you don't have to be helpless in the face of your emotions. You can use truth and reason (observations based on the principles of *logic*) to deflect, circumvent, or overrule emotions. Rather than allowing emotions to rule, you can *choose* to employ rational thinking to make decisions about how you will *choose* to feel about what someone else might be experiencing. In this chapter, we'll explore some ways you can bolster your emotional resilience.

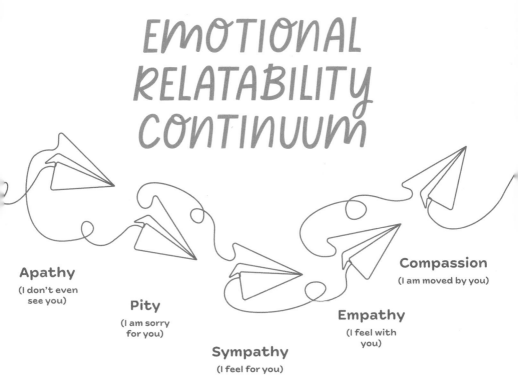

EMOTIONAL RELATABILITY CONTINUUM

Apathy
(I don't even see you)

Pity
(I am sorry for you)

Sympathy
(I feel for you)

Empathy
(I feel with you)

Compassion
(I am moved by you)

UNDERSTAND EMOTIONS AND HOW THEY WORK

Emotions may be difficult to manage, particularly when you're in hyper-empathy mode, but emotions are crucial to our survival. Just consider the following:

- **Emotions communicate valuable information to you and to those around you.** Often, we feel what we feel and can identify the emotion, long before we know *why* we're feeling it. Others can see our emotional reaction and be given an opportunity to respond appropriately.

- **Emotions prepare you to take whatever action is needed to support happy emotions or seek relief from painful emotions.** Fear tells you that you're in danger; anger tells you that someone or something is causing you pain; sadness tells you that you've lost something valuable and need to grieve; happiness tells you that you feel loved and supported and should seek similar experiences. See your emotions as transitory messengers.

- **Emotions deepen our experience with life and bolster intimacy.** Imagine how dull your life would feel if you didn't experience emotions.

- **Fear is almost always the root of problematic emotions.** When you're struggling with negative or hurtful emotions, ask yourself what you're *afraid* will happen.

- **You are not your emotions.** Emotions are an *experience* your body and mind are feeling. You are not an *angry person.* You are *experiencing anger.*

- **Emotions are transitory.** Ideally, you allow them to flow through you, then release them. What's caused the pain can be evaluated *after* the feeling has subsided.

Many empaths take on the emotional experiences of others and do not release them. If you do this consistently, it can negatively affect your emotional bandwidth, which can lead to overstimulation.

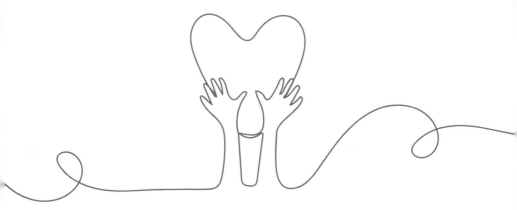

A person who knows to pause amidst an emotional crisis does better things for his inner self and the person in front of him.

—UDAYAKUMAR D.S., *Fearless and Free*

After assessing and thinking about the emotional tenets on the previous page, identify your most problematic emotions and reframe how you can view or approach them in a more productive manner. For example: "When I feel abandoned, rather than withdrawing further, I can see it as a sign that I need to ask for support."

1. _____

_____

2. _____

_____

3. _____

_____

4. _____

_____

5. _____

_____

Instead of resisting any emotion, the best way to dispel it is to enter it fully, embrace it and see through your resistance.

—DEEPAK CHOPRA, author

CULTIVATE EMOTIONAL INTELLIGENCE

Emotional intelligence (EQ) reflects your ability to identify, understand, and use your own emotions in positive ways to relieve stress and anxiety, communicate effectively, empathize with others, overcome challenges, and defuse conflict. When it comes to happiness and success in your relationships, career, and personal goals, researchers have found that your EQ matters just as much as your IQ (intelligence quotient). Emotional intelligence is reflected in how you:

Manage your emotions. You successfully manage any impulsive feelings and behaviors that occur in healthy ways; you often take initiative; you honor your commitments; you adapt well to changing circumstances.

Reflect self-awareness. You recognize your own emotions and how they affect your thoughts and behavior; you accept your strengths and weaknesses and feel confident about who you are in the world.

Exhibit social awareness. You notice and heed emotional cues; you both see and understand the emotions, needs, and concerns of other people (without taking them on); you feel comfortable in most social situations; you both see and work well within the power dynamics of a group or organization.

Maintain healthy relationships. You're able to develop and maintain strong, reciprocal, high-functioning relationships; you communicate clearly and inspire and influence others; you enjoy and benefit from teamwork; you know how to effectively manage conflict.

These are standards for you to pursue, and with conscious self-observation and application of the techniques in this book, you can significantly bolster your "emotional IQ."

How do you rate your progress on the signs of emotional intelligence
(EQ) from the previous page? Where do you need to focus? Be specific.

_____

_____

_____

_____

_____

_____

_____

_____

Brainstorm strategies for improving your EQ.

_____

_____

_____

_____

_____

_____

_____

_____

_____

_____

LEARN TO IDENTIFY PROBLEMATIC EMOTIONS

Highly sensitive people are particularly vulnerable to taking on other people's feelings to the point they suppress, deny, and even misinterpret their own feelings. You are so sensitive to what others need (and busy trying to provide it) that you lose sight of what *you* need, which often creates frustration, resentment, and anger. Eventually, your emotions will demand attention, bubble to the surface (or explode), and attach themselves to situations that have little relevance to what you're feeling.

How do you know when your emotions have become problematic?

- Your reaction is more intense than what the current situation warranted.

- You're so upset you can't identify what you're really feeling.

- Your emotional response feels habitual or like something you experienced long ago.

- You negatively assess your emotions, berate yourself for expressing them, and feel guilty for even feeling them.

- Your reaction seems disproportionate and uncontrollable.

- Even when the current crisis is resolved, you have trouble releasing the emotion.

Which of the previous have you experienced? Anything recently?

_____

_____

_____

_____

_____

_____

_____

_____

_____

_____

_____

She had a very inconvenient heart. It always insisted on feeling things ever so deeply.

—JOHN MARK GREEN,
She Had a Very Inconvenient Heart

What triggered it?

_____

_____

_____

_____

_____

_____

_____

_____

_____

_____

_____

_____

Was your response in proportion to and relevant to the situation?

_____

_____

_____

_____

_____

How could you have managed it better?

_____

_____

_____

_____

_____

_____

_____

_____

_____

_____

_____

_____

_____

_____

_____

_____

_____

_____

_____

_____

TAME YOUR EMOTIONS

The best way to heal your emotions is to offer yourself the following:

Self-compassion. Forgive yourself for having human emotions and be gentle with yourself when your emotions feel unmanageable.

Self-acceptance. Accept yourself as you are. Feel what you feel, while recognizing that your temporary feelings don't necessarily reflect who you are. Accept whatever you are feeling, welcome whatever insight is needed, appropriately express the underlying (real) emotion, and then release any unwanted emotions.

Time for introspection/reflection. Strong emotions convey essential knowledge about what's important to you that is or is not being met. Use them as the messengers they are and give yourself adequate time and space to reflect on what your emotions are trying to tell you.

GET COMFORTABLE WITH YOUR EMOTIONS

The following short quiz measures your level of emotional awareness. There are no right or wrong responses, only the opportunity to become better acquainted with your emotional responses.

Rarely   Occasionally   Often   Very Often   Almost Always

☐ ☐ ☐ ☐ ☐   Do your feelings flow, shifting from one emotion to another, in alignment with what you're experiencing in the moment?

☐ ☐ ☐ ☐ ☐   Do you experience distinct feelings and emotions, such as anger, sadness, love, and joy?

☐ ☐ ☐ ☐ ☐   Do you occasionally have intense feelings that are strong enough to capture both your own and others' attention but which you quickly recognize and address?

☐ ☐ ☐ ☐ ☐   Are overpowering emotions accompanied by physical sensations, such as stomach flutters, tightness in your chest, nausea, or headache that subside when you admit to and address the feelings?

☐ ☐ ☐ ☐ ☐   Do you avoid suppressing any physical revelation of what you're really feeling, because you feel comfortable when others know what you're feeling?

☐ ☐ ☐ ☐ ☐   Do you pay attention to and value your emotions as the messengers they are?

☐ ☐ ☐ ☐ ☐   Do you take your emotions into account when making decisions?

Obviously, if your answers tended toward "Very often" or "almost always," you are comfortable feeling your emotions but also manage them well (a good thing); if your answers tended toward "rarely" and "occasionally," you may have learned to tamp down, ignore, or even bury your emotions (a problematic thing). Because our early caregivers or teachers may have encouraged us to hide, ignore, or even fully suppress our feelings, many of us are disconnected from them—especially strong emotions such as anger, sadness, and fear. While it's possible to deny or numb your feelings, whether you're aware of having them or not, strong emotions will still occur, often persist, and fester when buried.

Identify the emotions that cause you the most anxiety.

1. _____

_____

2. _____

_____

3. _____

_____

4. _____

_____

5. _____

_____

Is there an emotion that frightens you or consistently sends you into a negative spiral?

_____

_____

_____

_____

_____

_____

_____

_____

Can you identify the root cause? (See page 60 to help assuage it.)

_____

_____

_____

_____

_____

_____

_____

When your emotions seem out of control or inappropriate to the situation, list ways you can calm yourself and view the situation more objectively (see page 117 if you need ideas).

1. _____

_____

2. _____

_____

3. _____

_____

4. _____

_____

5. _____

_____

SEE THE POSITIVES

Some of us have learned to hide what we consider unpleasant or undesirable emotions. However, even unpleasant emotions can have beneficial aspects. Sadness can support emotional healing, fear can trigger life-saving action, and anger can mobilize and inspire energy for change. Viewing all emotions as positive messengers will allow them to flow in and out with more ease.

You can't help what you feel, but you can help how you behave.

—MARGARET ATWOOD, *The Handmaid's Tale*

MANAGE YOUR EMOTIONS

A stressed-out empath needs a heightened ability to manage emotions. Ways to accomplish this include:

IDENTIFY THE CAUSE OF YOUR ANXIETY

Once you understand the root cause, ways to manage it usually become apparent. Whenever you feel overwhelmed or upset, take a few minutes to write about what's causing your anxiety. Once it's on the page, your mind will help you see it more objectively and develop strategies to address the situation.

FIND BALANCE BY MEDITATING

Meditation—focusing on slow breaths, releasing negative thoughts, and clearing your mind—helps you relax and makes room for solutions to occur. You can find a wealth of meditation guidance online; make use of it on a regular basis.

PRACTICE MINDFULNESS

Mindfulness helps you stay present and focused on the moment, which in turn helps you gain perspective and thus better control your emotions. Gift yourself ten minutes every day, or every other day, to mindfully meditate, where you're intensely aware of what you're feeling or sensing without self-judgment. Over time, you'll be able to employ it, at will, as a strategy. We discuss mindfulness meditation on page 122, but you can find a wealth of information on mindfulness, as well as many mindfulness meditations, online.

EAT NUTRITIOUSLY

Eating a healthy diet helps you feel better both physically and mentally. Create meal plans for a week that you know will nourish your mental health. Cut back on all foods that offer zero nutrition, that you know aren't good for you, or that make you feel bad.

GET ENOUGH SLEEP

Adequate, REM (restorative) sleep is essential to overall well-being. If you're not sleeping well, or at least seven hours each night, consult a medical professional, or do an internet search, for ways to improve your sleep habits—and then put them into motion. Some culprits might include too much screen time before bed, caffeine late in the day, or certain medications.

EXERCISE REGULARLY

Physical movement has been clinically proven to help dissipate stress and improve mood. Run, jog, or simply walk it off. Make ongoing exercise a habit.

JOURNAL ABOUT YOUR FEELINGS

When you experience worrisome thoughts and feelings, writing about them will help you objectively view, process, and release them. Journal on a regular basis to gain greater understanding of negative patterns and identify situations or people you need to address.

CONNECT WITH FRIENDS AND FAMILY MEMBERS

Talking to people who love you (as you are) helps you feel supported and less alone. Don't sit and stew; call someone.

EMPLOY NATURE THERAPY

Simply being in nature can help you stop obsessing and feel more relaxed and at peace. You don't need parks, rivers, or oceans. Go outside, look around, and admire the foliage, the sky, the breeze, the birdsong, or the flowers. Take off your shoes and walk in the grass.

FIND CREATIVE OUTLETS

Painting, writing, music, photography, knitting, and many other creative activities can help you express your emotions in a healthy way. You don't have to be proficient (or even good) or create anything anyone else has to see or evaluate. Do it for you, alone.

Nourishing yourself in a way that helps you blossom in the direction you want to go is attainable, and you are worth the effort.

—DEBORAH DAY, *Be Happy Now!*

Which three of the previous strategies—*that you're not already using*—
would work best for you? Write a few sentences below to show how
you'll put them into motion.

1. _____

_____

_____

_____

_____

2. _____

_____

_____

_____

_____

3. _____

_____

_____

_____

_____

Which of the previous strategies would work best when you're in hyper-empathy mode? Choose three strategies you've not used often and write about how and when you might implement them.

1. _____

_____

_____

_____

_____

_____

2. _____

_____

_____

_____

_____

_____

3. _____

_____

_____

_____

_____

_____

USE MINDFULNESS TO CALM AND CLARIFY

According to Susan M. Orsillo, PhD, and Lizabeth Roemer, PhD, authors of *The Mindful Way through Anxiety*, mindfulness is useful in managing emotions because it's a method you can use to purposefully expand your attention to take in both what is happening inside—your thoughts, feelings, physical sensations—and what is happening around you. Regular practice helps you bring an honest curiosity to your experiences and gain a fresh perspective on thoughts, feelings, people, and situations. The more you practice mindfulness, initially by meditating for five to ten minutes a day, the better you'll become at objectively viewing people and situations (and your reactions); you will thereby be able to choose how you respond, in the moment things happen.

Begin by sitting cross-legged on a cushion; use a pillow to slightly elevate your buttocks, use both legs for balance, and straighten your spine. You can also sit on a chair, with your feet flat on the floor. Place both palms down on your thighs or bring your hands together on your lap.

To begin, set a timer for five minutes, close your eyes (or stare at a focus point on the floor in front of you), and breathe slowly in and out, focusing solely on your breath, noticing the physical sensation of your breath entering and exiting. Clear your mind of any thoughts and your body of any feelings that arise. Don't judge them or the fact you are struggling to stay focused. Simply notice thoughts or feelings, then view them as butterflies that you promptly release to the sky. The goal is to improve your ability to both calm yourself and focus purely on what's happening *in the moment*.

If you practice this sort of simple mindfulness five days a week for several weeks, you will begin to notice an improved ability to focus and to notice what you are feeling and thinking in the moment—and thereby better manage your emotions. As you progress, you can choose from a wide assortment of online mindfulness meditations.

TRY A SELF-COMPASSION MINDFULNESS MEDITATION

When you are settled in position and your breathing is slow and steady, think back to a time when you felt angry or disrespected. Sans any judgment, conjure any images, thoughts, feelings, or sensations that happened in *that past* moment; then notice what images, thoughts, feelings, or sensations arise in *this current* moment. Stay with the memory until it feels resolved, then let it float away. Offer yourself compassion for what happened in the past, how you responded, and any feelings you may have retained.

When you did this meditation, which memory did you recall?

_____

_____

_____

_____

_____

_____

_____

_____

_____

_____

_____

_____

What thoughts and feelings did you experience when the situation or event first happened? What tripped you up?

_____

_____

_____

_____

_____

_____

_____

_____

When you conjured the memory, did you feel the same feelings? Think the same thoughts? How did it change?

_____

_____

_____

_____

_____

_____

_____

_____

TRY AFFECT LABELING

According to a study reported in *Emotion Review*, one way to better manage unruly emotions is to engage in affect labeling. Essentially, you pause to self-reflect on exactly what you are feeling (and perhaps what the person in front of you is feeling) and then put it into words. Doing so has been shown to reduce emotional reactivity and calm any physiological responses. When you pause to recognize and name what you're feeling, in the moment, you are engaging in dispositional mindfulness— awareness that involves paying attention to our thoughts and feelings in the present moment without judgment—by offering:

- Distraction
- Self-reflection
- Clarification
- Validation
- Reappraisal
- Reduced uncertainty

All of which means that you engage your conscious thinking brain (prefrontal cortex) to recognize and verbalize what you are feeling and tamp down emotional reactivity stemming from your unconscious brain's alarm system (amygdala). The next time your emotions feel out of control, pause to try affect labeling by first recognizing, then putting into words exactly what you are feeling.

During the self-compassion meditation, did you long to push certain feelings aside? Which feelings and why?

_____

_____

_____

_____

_____

_____

_____

When you re-experienced intense emotions, how did this feel in your body?

_____

_____

_____

_____

_____

_____

_____

Were you able to look at the past event or situation with fresh eyes, thereby gaining greater clarity? Would you react differently now?

_____

_____

_____

_____

_____

_____

_____

_____

Were you able to release any judgment about how you felt or reacted at the time, and now? Did you forgive yourself for the past and offer yourself compassion and understanding?

_____

_____

_____

_____

_____

_____

_____

_____

PRACTICE EMOTIONAL MASTERY

Choose a time when you feel stressed or angry, but only when the stakes are low, such as during the dreaded task of scrubbing a bathroom or getting stuck in endless traffic. Simply allow yourself to feel the frustration or anger, and then notice how this unleashed emotion affects your mind and body. Feel the impact, then release it. Remember to also experiment with joy, love, and happiness. The goal is to feel, recognize, and receive any messages, then honor and release your emotions.

When you are joyful, when you say yes to life and have fun and project positivity all around you, you become a sun in the center of every constellation, and people want to be near you.

—SHANNON L. ALDER, inspirational author

REALITY CHECK NEGATIVE THOUGHTS

According to Mark R. Leary, author of *The Curse of the Self*, when stressed, we tend to exaggerate how bad things are, which generates an unnecessary string of negative thoughts. Apparently, when stressed, our brains are not good at distinguishing between things that need immediate attention, like the house is on fire, and things that don't require an immediate, drastic response.

Leary recommends that you try *temporal distancing*, pausing to imagine yourself in the future. Not only can you simply imagine a time when everything you're stressing about has worked out, you can also *reality check* current negative thoughts. It's as easy as pausing for a few seconds to imagine whether the current crisis is likely to matter in a month, a year, or ten years. Leary suggests asking yourself: "Is this going to make a difference to my overall life?" With many sources of stress, the answer is likely no. "The big lesson you learn is that the quality of your life is so dependent on how you're thinking," Leary notes, "and we can't always trust our evaluation of our thoughts."

What are you stressing about currently? Write down any and all negative thoughts related to what you're perceiving as a problem.

_____

_____

_____

_____

_____

_____

My negative thoughts are:

1. _____

_____

2. _____

_____

3. _____

_____

4. _____

_____

5. _____

_____

My negative feelings are:

1. _____

_____

2. _____

_____

3. _____

_____

4. _____

_____

5. _____

Now, evaluate the situation causing you stress and answer Leary's question: "Is this going to make a difference to my overall life?" Are the negative thoughts you're having a trustworthy evaluation? If not, rephrase and reframe until you see the situation in a new light.

My newly positive thoughts are:

1. _____

_____

2. _____

_____

3. _____

_____

4. _____

_____

5. _____

_____

My newly positive feelings are:

1. _____

_____

2. _____

_____

3. _____

_____

4. _____

_____

5. _____

_____

Setting boundaries is about learning to take care of ourselves, no matter what happens, no matter where we go, or who we're with. Boundaries are rooted in our beliefs about what we deserve and don't deserve. Boundaries originate from a deeper sense of our personal rights—especially the right we have to be ourselves. Boundaries emerge as we learn to value, trust, and listen to ourselves. Boundaries naturally flow from our convictions that what we want, need, like, and dislike is important.

—MELODY BEATTIE, *Codependent No More*

Chapter 6

LEARN TO SET BOUNDARIES

According to the authors of *Boundaries for Your Soul*, Alison Cook, PhD, and Kimberly Miller, boundaries are borders or limits of who you are and what you do, and what behaviors (your own and those of others) you will and will not accept. They are a way to honor your individuality and the individuality of others. And, if you want to feel empowered, they are also a necessity for empaths.

Dr. Cook and Miller use an external boundary as an illustration of the concept: When talking face-to-face with someone, if a person stands too close, you may feel overwhelmed and need to take a step or two back; but if you move too far away, you may feel too removed and lose intimacy. The authors see setting boundaries as a moveable line that you establish to maintain and support your comfort level, and this could apply to both physical and emotional boundaries. You can move closer or step farther away until you find what feels like a comfortable distance.

PHYSICAL

| Too Close | Comfortable Distance | Too Far |

EMOTIONAL

| Too Apathic | Balanced Empathy | Too Enmeshed |

TYPES OF BOUNDARIES

Boundaries are arbitrary guidelines we establish to set parameters for how we will allow others to treat us, as well as how we will protect and honor ourselves. Sometimes you need physical boundaries, and if they aren't possible, you can use other boundaries to protect or nourish yourself. When it comes to setting boundaries, here are five to consider:

1. Mental: Use your high-functioning mind to establish your mental boundaries: know what matters most, what you truly believe, then hold firm to them. Don't allow others to sway you, no matter how hard they try.

2. Emotional: Choose relationships and work environments carefully. Limit exposure to anyone toxic. Allow others to feel what they feel but also be who *you* are. Walk away from anyone who doesn't respect your boundaries or abuses you.

3. Verbal: Choose your words and what you convey to others carefully. Make what you say be what you believe. Protect self-talk (what you say to yourself about yourself). Do not allow anyone to verbally insult or offend you.

4. Physical: Choose activities that support and nurture your highly sensitive nature. Strictly limit or stop being around anything that offends your sensibilities and causes psychic distress. When that's not possible, set boundaries for interactions; make time to prepare, endure, recoup, and restore; and practice regular self-care.

5. Spiritual: Honor your unique soul on a daily basis. Create rituals and methods that will both support your sensitive nature and offer more protection to your most essential self. (See Chapter 7.)

As a highly sensitive person, you are likely adept at focusing on others, losing sight of what you need. When you ignore or lose sight of your needs, it becomes harder to know what they are or even how to voice them. Setting boundaries is a way for those around you to take responsibility for their feelings, and for you to address yours.

> **I think so often what people misunderstand about boundaries is that the point of setting them is not to change other people's behavior or convince them to value different things— it's to advocate for yourself, regardless of how they respond.**
>
> **—DANIELL KOEPKE, *Daring to Take Up Space***

Which of the previous boundaries do you have trouble setting or keeping?

_____

_____

_____

_____

_____

_____

_____

_____

_____

List at least five ways others do not honor your boundaries.

1. _____

_____

2. _____

_____

3. _____

_____

4. _____

_____

5. _____

_____

Establish new boundaries for situations you want to avoid, or people who make a habit of disrespecting you.

1. _____

_____

2. _____

_____

3. _____

_____

4. _____

_____

5. _____

_____

> ## "People with good boundaries quickly address infractions and do not put up with repeated patterns of hurtful or impossible behavior.
>
> —HENRY CLOUD, PhD, *The Law of Happiness*

ESTABLISH YOUR BOUNDARIES

Setting boundaries is not about pushing others away; it's about honoring who you are and what you need. It's about limiting anything that causes you undue distress and safeguarding your inner peace. Consider how you need to safeguard your inner self as you answer the following questions:

What basic tenets about living life are so essential to your wellbeing you can't live without them? Which beliefs support your highly sensitive nature?

_____

_____

_____

_____

_____

_____

_____

_____

_____

_____

_____

_____

_____

_____

What are things said or done that violate your sense of what's right, moral, productive, or supportive? What offends your sensibility? What causes moral outrage? What can you simply not tolerate?

_____

_____

_____

_____

_____

_____

_____

_____

_____

_____

_____

_____

_____

_____

_____

_____

_____

_____

_____

_____

_____

As empaths, we are not here
to be sponges or enablers. We
are here to be helpers, guides,
and supporters. The very best
thing we can do for others
isn't soaking up their pain,
it is actually holding space
for them. Holding space for
a person means giving them
the room to grieve or vent
while still maintaining our own
boundaries.

—ALETHEIA LUNA AND MATEO SOL, *Awakened Empath*

What activities drain your positive energy and leave you feeling depleted? Which ones are essential or must be endured, for now? How can you protect yourself until you can find more supportive environments or activities?

_____

_____

_____

_____

_____

_____

_____

_____

_____

_____

_____

_____

_____

_____

_____

_____

BOUNDARY SETTING BASICS

Things that are NOT your responsibility:

- Anticipating someone else's needs

- Feeling other people's feelings

- Sacrificing yourself to please others

- Indulging someone else's injurious behavior

- Being the only one trying to make it work

- Being the one who is always compromising

- Healing anyone else's emotional pain

Things that are YOUR responsibility:

- Recognizing and fulfilling your needs and desires

- Respecting and protecting your boundaries, time, and energy

- Being your authentic self at all times

- Protecting yourself from abuse or those who don't respect you

- Never agreeing to something that doesn't align with your values

- Pausing to assess before automatically saying "yes"

- Healing your own emotional wounds

What activities feed or strengthen your positive energy and fire you up? List ways you can weave more of these activities into your current and future life.

_____

_____

_____

_____

_____

_____

_____

_____

_____

_____

_____

_____

_____

_____

_____

_____

_____

_____

Who can't see who you are and what you need or consistently drains your energy? Have you set boundaries with them? Do they consistently breach your boundaries? How can you enforce your boundaries or limit exposure to them?

_____

_____

_____

_____

_____

_____

_____

_____

_____

_____

_____

_____

_____

_____

_____

_____

_____

_____

NO MORE THIRD CHANCES

According to relationship expert Erin Leonard, PhD, an individual who has hurt, betrayed, or disrespected you—*if* they sincerely apologize and convey a clear understanding of how their mistake affected you—may deserve a second chance. However, if hurtful action occurs again (showing a consistent lack of empathy and authentic accountability), offering more chances to this individual may not be wise. If the person does not feel remorse and does not make efforts *not to repeat* the same hurtful behavior, they are far more likely to reoffend.

Who supports who you are and what you need in your life? Are you spending enough time with them, or reaching out to them enough? Where can you find even more people on the same wavelength? What can you do to generate more support?

KNOW YOUR BASIC HUMAN RIGHTS

According to Judith Orloff, MD, author of *The Empath's Survival Guide* and *The Genius of Empathy*, highly sensitive people may lose sight of what should be their basic human rights and thus have difficulty setting and maintaining boundaries. She lists four essential rights that you can use as mantras to keep focus on yourself and your needs, and thereby prevent or lessen feeling overwhelmed. If you're struggling, write the following four rights (or your own) on notecards, tape them around your house, or speak them into your phone recorder as reminders:

- I have the right to say a loving and positive "no" or "no thank-you."

- I have the right to set limits on how long I listen to people's problems.

- I have the right to rest and not be always available to everyone.

- I have the right to quiet peacefulness in my home and in my heart.

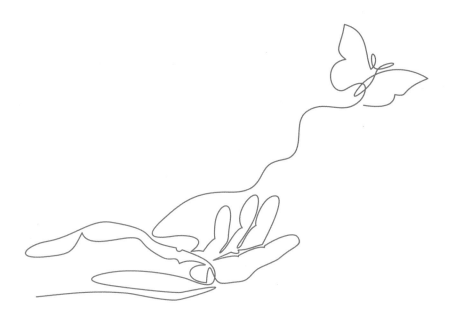

Empathy has no script. There is no right way or wrong way to do it. It's simply listening, holding space, withholding judgment, emotionally connecting, and communicating that incredibly healing message of 'You're not alone.'

—BRENÉ BROWN, PhD, *Daring Greatly*

What do you now understand to be your basic rights when it comes to being emotionally sensitive to others? Which ones do you need to bolster?

_____

_____

_____

_____

_____

_____

_____

What can you specifically do to make sure you honor and safeguard your basic rights?

_____

_____

_____

_____

_____

_____

_____

_____

_____

One of the criticisms I've faced over the years is that I'm not aggressive enough or assertive enough or maybe somehow because I'm empathetic, it means I'm weak. I totally rebel against that. I refuse to believe that you cannot be both compassionate and strong.

—JACINDA ARDERN, 40th prime minister of New Zealand

LOVE YOURSELF AS YOU ARE

Empaths are so busy offering loving support to others that they often forget to extend equal attention, compassion, kindness, and generosity to themselves. Alexandra Elle, author of *How We Heal*, says highly sensitive people are adept at offering love to others but often need "stepping-stones" to learn how to offer themselves love. She suggests the following exercise:

Set a timer for ten minutes and write a list of how others have shown, or currently show, their love for you. Specify what they love about you and how they show it.

1. _____

2. _____

3. _____

4. _____

5. _____

6. _____

7. _____

8. _____

9. _____

10. _____

Set a timer again for ten minutes and write a list of everything *you* love about yourself. If this feels too hard (and it often is for empaths), write a list of what you *want* to love about yourself.

1. _____

_____

2. _____

_____

3. _____

_____

4. _____

_____

5. _____

_____

6. _____

_____

7. _____

_____

8. _____

_____

9. _____

_____

10. _____

_____

In the previous exercise, you likely discovered that you need "stepping-stones" to help you learn how to offer yourself the same kind of protection, compassion, and love you offer to others.

Using the illustration that follows, use the bubbles to write down "stepping-stones" of small acts of self-love you can do to show yourself compassion, understanding, love, and acceptance. Examples might look like:

Holding firm to my boundaries with family

Taking one night a week just for me

Walking away from unhealthy relationships

Speaking with clarity about what I want and need

SELF-LOVE STEPPING-STONES

Being honest with myself and others

Listening with compassion; trusting others to deal with their emotions

SELF-LOVE STEPPING-STONES

LEARN TO SELF-SOOTHE

When their caregivers aren't available or don't respond promptly, most infants learn to self-soothe (which is a good skill to learn!). As adults, when our emotions seem out of control or we feel burned out, we can consciously choose self-soothing activities. Consider the following options:

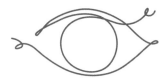

Sight:
Dim the lights or light a candle.
Look at soothing colors or images.
Put on a warm or fragrant eye mask.
Find images you love on Pinterest.

Sound:
Go out in nature and listen to birds.
Find a guided meditation online.
Listen to a soothing CD.
Call a loved one so you can hear their voice.

Touch:
Lie under a soft or weighted blanket.
Massage your shoulders and neck.
Take a hot or cold shower.
Take a bubble bath.

Smell:

Light a fragment candle, such as soothing lavender.

Cook something that creates smells you love.

Go outside for fresh air.

Smell something that brings you joy, like clean laundry or your pet's fur.

Taste:

Have a cup of herbal tea.

Savor eating something that comforts you.

Eat something that is healthy and nourishing.

Allow yourself to eat something your inner child would love.

Choose something in each of the categories on the previous page that you can use to self-soothe. If necessary, put the list on your refrigerator to remind you to use them the next time you feel stressed or anxious.

Sight _____

_____

_____

_____

Sound _____

_____

_____

_____

Touch _____

_____

_____

_____

Smell _____

_____

_____

_____

Taste _____

_____

_____

_____

What else could you specifically do to self-soothe? (Pick activities, sights, and sounds that calm and comfort you.)

1. _____

_____

_____

_____

2. _____

_____

_____

_____

3. _____

_____

_____

_____

4. _____

_____

_____

_____

5. _____

_____

_____

_____

The ethereal beauty of a dandelion, the shift of a season, the climax of a song, or a certain stirring scent can awaken such wonder they'll become your very breath itself—moving through you as fuel does to fire and wind does to waves.

—VICTORIA ERICKSON, poet

EMBRACE THE SCIENCE OF HAPPINESS

When you're happy, it's easier to maintain your boundaries and protect your positive state of mind. In *The Science of Happiness*, Bruce Hood, PhD, lists seven "happiness hacks" you can use to improve your state of mind and maintain it:

1. Perform acts of kindness.
2. Increase social connections, including initiating conversations with strangers.
3. Savor your experiences.
4. Deliberately draw your attention to the positive events and aspects of your day.
5. Practice feeling grateful and thanking others for their kindnesses.
6. Be physically active.
7. Explore mindfulness or other meditation techniques.

Which of the above mood boosters are you currently doing?

_____

_____

_____

_____

_____

_____

_____

_____

_____

Which mood boosters could you practice more often?

_____

_____

_____

_____

_____

_____

_____

_____

What else could serve as your unique "happiness hacks"?

1. _____

_____

2. _____

_____

3. _____

_____

4. _____

_____

5. _____

_____

Be soft. Do not let the world
make you hard. Do not let
pain make you hate. Do not let
bitterness steal your sweetness.
Take pride that even though the
rest of the world may disagree,
you still believe it to be a
beautiful place.

—KURT VONNEGUT, novelist

INSTEAD OF FOMO, TRY JOMO

The barrage of idyllic (and often unrealistic) images one sees on social media can create FOMO (Fear of Missing Out), which isn't helpful. But you can embrace what social scientist Tali Gazit, PhD, associate professor of Information Science at Bar-Ilan University in Israel, calls JOMO (*Joy of Missing Out*). She says it's as easy as jettisoning time on social media (or your phone) and then *cultivating* opportunities to disconnect and recharge. It's about *inviting joy* in. Three simple ways to start:

1. Consistently set aside time each day to log off and enjoy being unavailable.
2. Turn off notifications; set daily time limits for perusing social media, endlessly scrolling, or playing games; and power off your phone at night.
3. Be mindful when scrolling or gaming (that is, be aware of what you're feeling and thinking). If it's dampening your mood, log off!

"JOMO is actually being able to be in the here and now, to be able to enjoy what you are doing now, without looking left and right and being jealous or anxious about missing something," she notes.

LEARN TO EMBRACE AWE

Dacher Keltner, PhD, author of *Awe*, says awe is not considered a "basic emotion" but "is its own thing." He notes that our bodies make a different sound and our faces show a different expression when we are experiencing awe than when we are feeling joy, contentment, or fear.

Awe activates the vagal nerves, clusters of neurons in the spinal cord that regulate various bodily functions, and thereby slows our heart rate, relieves digestion, and deepens breathing. Awe also deactivates the default mode network in our brains (involved in how we perceive ourselves), which seems to quiet negative self-talk and minimize self-preoccupation. It also calms down our nervous system and triggers the release of oxytocin, the "love" hormone that promotes trust and bonding.

Dr. Keltner describes awe as "the feeling of being in the presence of something vast that transcends your understanding of the world." Ways to experience awe include:

- traveling to exotic locations and exploring unique cultures;

- opening yourself to new experiences where you live;

- challenging your intellect or creative abilities;

- viewing or exploring awe-inspiring landscapes or visual art;

- reading and savoring poetry or other inspirational literary works;

- attentively listening to music that stirs something meaningful inside you;

- viewing movies, documentaries, or plays that move you;

- noticing and feeling inspired by acts of love or charity, especially toward strangers;

- practicing deep contemplation via meditation or mindfulness.

List three specific ways you have experienced awe in the past.

1. _____

_____

_____

2. _____

_____

_____

3. _____

_____

_____

List three specific things you can do to experience more awe on a regular basis.

1. _____

_____

_____

2. _____

_____

_____

3. _____

_____

_____

If the sight of the blue skies fills you with joy, if a blade of grass springing up in the fields has power to move you, if the simple things of nature have a message that you understand, rejoice, for your soul is alive.

—ELEONORA DUSE, actress

What you may not realize is that hiding just below the surface of this burden is a shiny pearl.

—APRIL SNOW, *Find Your Strength*

Chapter 7

EMBRACE
PSYCHIC SHIELDING

As an empath, your psychic abilities and susceptibility to taking on other people's energy are easily and frequently stimulated and often overworked. To maintain the strength and clarity needed to heal your traumas, set boundaries, and manage your emotions, you need to nurture, protect, and recharge your intuition, your energy, and your spirit. In this chapter, we'll offer ways you can protect your psychic energy and refresh your spirit.

CONNECT TO THE EARTH

When stressed, it's always good to connect to the earth. One of the best ways to do this is to literally use the ground under your feet. Simply find a quiet spot outside, take off your shoes and socks, either stand or sit, and firmly plant your feet on the ground. Visualize your energy traveling down into the earth, then envision its rooted, calming, grounding effect flowing back up through your body. If you can't literally go outside in the moment, once you've practiced this a few times, you'll be able to achieve the same effect indoors.

The divine self guides you always, and the luminous light of the soul protects you. Have no fear.

—ANTHON ST. MAARTEN, *Divine Living*

PROTECT YOUR ENERGY WITH CRYSTALS

Crystals, when simply held or worn, can attract positive energy and dissipate unwanted negative energy around you. You can also use them in meditation to heal, energize, and repel or attract energy. Before you use them, choose the one(s) most appropriate for what you need, stand in daylight with it in the palm of your hand, and state what you desire, such as: "I need this selenite to help me cleanse my surroundings." Some crystals considered particularly helpful for empaths include the following:

Black tourmaline absorbs electromagnetic frequencies and makes the perfect talisman to wear around your neck.

Selenite helps protect empaths by cleansing everything in its surroundings, and itself.

Amethyst repels negative energies and invites positive ones. It also boosts your psychic ability, which will increase confidence in your ability to psychically protect yourself.

Citrine balances your emotions, increases confidence, and repels negativity.

Obsidian repairs a damaged or bombarded aura and can be used to ward off future negativity.

Black jade bolsters intuition, which helps you recognize negative people and situations.

Pyrite has a calming effect on the body and the mind.

Smithsonite helps you relax and calm you down after a hectic day.

Clear quartz shields you from negative energies and attracts positive energies.

Note: Every so often, cleanse and recharge your crystals by placing them on a windowsill where they can absorb moonlight overnight. You can also cover them with sea salt and let them sit overnight, then cleanse them. Or you can simply rinse them in water, but make sure you check the properties of your crystal first, as some don't like water. (To find out each crystal's unique qualities and needs, visit websites such as Unearthedstore.com.)

GUARD YOUR SPIRIT WITH A PSYCHIC PROTECTION JAR

Because empaths are deeply sensitive to energy, creating a "protection jar" is one way to encourage psychic shielding. Some items that might be useful include the following:

Rosemary purifies your environment and removes negativity. Because it represents "new beginnings," use it when opening yourself up to new opportunities or trying to break unhealthy habits.

Sage is a natural purifier that can cleanse your energy and the air around you. It fosters more restful sleep.

Mint protects your home from negativity and attracts abundance. Some Middle Eastern cultures use it to remove negative energies and invite in helpful spirits.

Cinnamon reminds us of a comforting warm fire and the joy of holidays, providing an uplifting energy boost.

Sea salt or black salt absorbs negative energies and drives away unwanted spirits.

Basil is a powerful protective herb, thought to appease deities and ward off evil spirits.

Whole cloves bring mental clarity, dispel negativity, and encourage a sense of release.

Black pepper wards off negative influences, helps you release jealous or vindictive thoughts, and forms a powerful protective barrier around your home.

Dried bay leaf is strongly connected with good luck, empowerment, and financial protection.

Sweet grass cleanses auras, objects, and spaces. Some Native American cultures braid it, dry it, and then burn it to attract positivity and provide protection for the tribe.

Lavender has calming properties and relieves stress. It can also protect against abuse, psychic attacks, and nightmares, and it can attract good luck into your life.

Sunflower petals will help you see the truth in any situation and provide protection, vibrancy, and the empowerment to face any situation (ideal for empaths!).

Mullein instills courage, attracts love, and provides protection by giving you courage to face your enemies.

Cayenne pepper banishes or reverses negative emotions and promotes warmth in relationships. Adding a small cayenne pepper (or ground pepper) to your spirit jar enhances all the other ingredients' protective powers.

Hematite is a grounding stone that bolsters inner peace and the strength needed to heal old wounds.

Black tourmaline provides a protective shield that absorbs and repels negative energies. It also transforms anxious feelings into positive ones.

Clear quartz dispels negativity, while attracting positivity. It enhances the energy flow within your body, which fosters a more positive state of mind.

Thoroughly wash and dry any size jar, then smudge it with sage or another suitable herb (see right). Make sure the jar is fully dried before adding your ingredients. Start with the heavier items and, as you add each item, focus deeply on your intentions. You can even use mantras to clearly invite the desired effect:

- *This sage will cleanse the air around me and foster healing sleep.*
- *These sunflower petals will help me see the truth in all situations.*
- *This hematite will help me feel protected and empowered to take on any challenge.*

Once the jar is full, screw the lid on tightly, seal it with melted wax, and place it somewhere you can see it often and invite its protection.

SMUDGE OUT NEGATIVITY

Native Americans long regarded burning white sage herbal bundles as a powerful cleansing tool, and these bundles are widely available today. Simply light the sage bundle (make sure you also have a fireproof bowl to catch ashes); hold the smoking herb bundle close to your body (but not too close); then close your eyes, and allow the smoke to flow over and around you. Envision its cleansing energy inside you and around you. Wave it in and around your empty protection jar. Then, walk around your living space waving the smudge stick, but be sure to open a window so any unwanted negativity has an escape hatch! If you don't like the smell of sage, try lavender, Palo Santo, sandalwoods, or incense sticks.

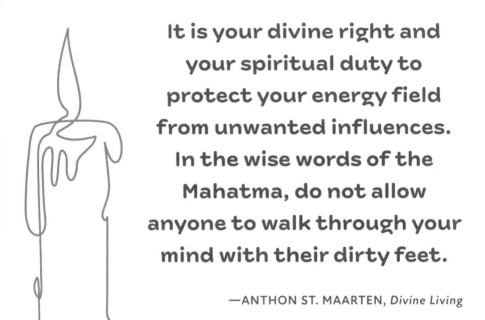

It is your divine right and your spiritual duty to protect your energy field from unwanted influences. In the wise words of the Mahatma, do not allow anyone to walk through your mind with their dirty feet.

—ANTHON ST. MAARTEN, *Divine Living*

NURTURE YOUR SOUL WITH A SACRED ALTAR

Choose a space in your home where you can place items that hold deep meaning for you and that "speak" to your soul. Perhaps use a special decorative cloth, candles, incense, pictures, and any objects that hold particular meaning, such as stones, crystals, feathers, oracle cards, rattles, singing bowls, or anything else that you can see, hold, or hear that will calm your spirit. This would create a space for meditation, as well as a space to simply calm your breathing and refocus. Light a candle and sit quietly at your personal altar once a day, or as often as you can. Over time, simply sitting in your sacred space can restore your energy.

RESTORE ENERGY WITH SOUND

While empaths are particularly sensitive to loud sounds or cacophonies of sound, sound *can* be your best friend. When it's kept at a low volume or features soothing qualities, sound can be as relaxing as a warm, candlelit bath.

SOUND MEDITATION

Sound therapy can significantly alter brainwaves, changing agitated wave patterns to exceptionally calm wave forms. As your brainwaves slow down, you shift from an active state to a more relaxed, dreamlike state. Many sounds can be soothing: Tibetan bowls, crystal bowls, rattles, rain sticks, and even tuning forks can be healing. Binaural beats—listening to two different programmed frequencies at the same time—can soothe nerves, as will sound meditations, both of which you can find online.

SOUND BATH

Sound baths are a meditative practice that uses evocative music to create an immersive sound that fills the room and vibrates your body. It's said to induce relaxation and help you release stress, anxiety, or other worries and concerns. Many feel deeply relaxed after sound baths, which may also have health benefits. Emerging research suggests sound therapy may lower stress hormones, improve mood, and reduce pain.

To achieve maximum benefit, eliminate all other distractions, choose music that holds meaning to you, and play it at a volume high enough to fill the room and send vibrations through your body. Sit back and soak up the sound.

SOOTHE NERVES WITH AROMATHERAPY

Inhaling or using a diffuser to breathe in the scents of essential oils can be very soothing. You can also: use scented candles; rub the oils on your body (a couple drops mixed with a carrier oil such as coconut, grapeseed, or apricot kernel oil); or add a couple drops to your bath—or use a scented bath bomb. The more you use oils to soothe you, the more the scent will imprint and later automatically induce the desired effect. Here are ten essential oils that offer healing and calming benefits for empaths:

Lavender has a calming effect, lessens worry, and improves sleep.

Black spruce brings harmony and peace to a troubled mind.

Chamomile helps calm and relax your body, especially your stomach.

Sage reduces cortisol, the stress hormone, and lessens anxiety.

Jasmine activates GABA, a neurotransmitter that reduces anxiety.

Rosemary reduces stress, fatigue, and mental exhaustion.

Lemon rejuvenates, increases serotonin and dopamine (feel-good brain chemicals).

Marjoram provides psychological protection by calming the mind and reducing anxiety.

Frankincense can be paired with lavender and bergamot to tamp down anxiety.

Vetiver quiets the mind, relieves stress and anxiety.

VISUALIZE A SHIELD

Envisioning a shield around us is one way to ward off unwanted emotions. Simply close your eyes and imagine a bright white light surrounding you. Feel it getting brighter and more vivid, enveloping you so thoroughly, you allow its warmth to penetrate through to your muscles and your mind. Imagine that this shield is dissipating all the dark or negative places in your mind and body. Then envision the light as an invisible shield that will repel unwanted emotions. When you are ready, open your eyes and enjoy feeling both lighter and protected. Use this image whenever you feel like your boundaries are being breached.

VALIDATE INTUITION WITH ORACLE CARDS

Whether it's the I Ching, tarot, angels, or healing mantras, you can find all sorts of oracle cards designed to facilitate self-reflection and insight. These can be a helpful tool for accessing your intuition, which may have important messages. Some people use them as a prompt for meditation or journaling. You can find hundreds of selections online.

GROUND YOUR ENERGY WITH YOGA

Some simple yoga poses, such as those that follow, can be a fast, effective way to ground your energy and restore your spirit. Holding the poses, while slowly breathing in and out, helps you slow down, focus, and stretch your body, all of which will help you feel grounded.

LEGS UP THE WALL

Legs up the wall (viparita karani) is an easy pose to get your started. Find a place where you can sit with your buttocks about 18 inches from a wall. Lie back, then slowly push your legs up the wall until they are straight. Rest your hands effortlessly alongside your body. While in this position, ensure you don't stress your legs or back. Breathe for five to ten minutes, then slowly lower your legs.

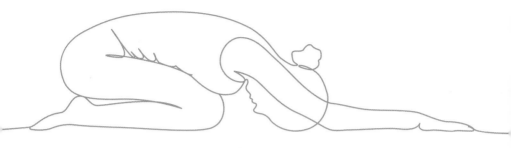

CHILD'S POSE

Child's pose *(balasana)* resembles the fetal position of a child in the womb. Sit on your heels with your knees spread apart and lean forward, gently pushing your belly down between your legs until it's almost touching the floor. Stretch your hands forward or rest them next to your body. If needed, add a bolster or pillow in front of your legs before coming into the position and a pillow under your forehead. Breathe slowly in and out as you hold the pose for five minutes. This pose will not only ground you but help you feel comforted and nourished.

TREE POSE

Tree pose *(vrikshasana)* will ground your energy. Stand with your legs shoulder-width apart. Lift your right foot, bring its knee out to the side, then place your foot on your left leg close to the knee (or wherever is comfortable). Lift both arms straight above your head and clasp or put your hands together. If you're able to, look up at your hands while maintaining balance. Breathe in and out slowly for a few minutes. Repeat with the other leg.

BALANCE YOUR ENERGY WITH TAI CHI

The ancient practice of tai chi is based on qigong and internal Chinese martial arts, those that relate to spiritual, mental, or qi (vital energy). Tai chi promotes inner peace and spiritual recovery. The central premise is learning to consciously use your power to move through pain, embracing what is most feared and opening what has been closed. Tai chi not only teaches you how to "flow," it helps you release everything that hasn't worked. Here's how a regular tai chi practice can help:

- It encourages the smooth flow of your life energy (qi) throughout your body.

- It enhances mindfulness by increasing awareness of how your mind operates, which will help you claim and consciously use your mental powers for healing.

- It strengthens your body and helps you start anew each day.

- It helps you navigate your emotions, take control, and heal emotional wounds.

- It reduces stress, leading to a journey within, where peace and calm exist.

AFTERWORD

Now that we've gone on the long journey together, you not only have a better understanding of why you've been feeling overwhelmed, but you now have an arsenal of tools to recognize when you're in hyper-empathy mode, identify your vulnerabilities, rein in your empathy (when needed), better manage your emotions, set boundaries, and protect your spirit. You can refer to this workbook whenever you feel overwhelmed—and get right back on track.

Take a moment to reflect on your journey and write about what impacted you the most. Perhaps it's the need to heal or set boundaries?

_____

_____

_____

_____

_____

_____

_____

_____

_____

_____

_____

_____

_____

_____

_____

What insights have you gained?

_____

_____

_____

_____

_____

_____

_____

_____

How will you put what you've learned into action?

_____

_____

_____

_____

_____

_____

_____

_____

RESOURCES

Beattie, Melody. *Codependent No More: How to Stop Controlling Others and Start Caring for Yourself*, Spiegel & Grau, 2022.

Bidwell Smith, Claire. *Anxiety: The Missing Stage of Grief*, Hachette, 2013.

Bloom, Paul. *Against Empathy: The Case for Rational Compassion*, HarperCollins, 2016.

Boyle, Sherianna. *Energy in Action: The Power of Emotions and Intuition to Cultivate Peace and Freedom*, Sounds True, 2023.

Brown, Brené, PhD. *Daring Greatly: How the Courage to Be Vulnerable Transforms the Way We Live, Love, Parent, and Lead*, Avery, 2015.

Campos, Sydney. *The Empath Experience: What to Do When You Feel Everything*, Adams Media, 2018.

Cloud, Henry. *The Law of Happiness: How Spiritual Wisdom and Modern Science Can Change Your Life*, Howard Books, 2011.

Cook, Alison, PhD, and Kimerly Miller. *Boundaries for Your Soul: How to Turn Overwhelming Thoughts and Feelings into Your Greatest Allies*, Nelson Books, 2018.

Delony, John. *Redefining Anxiety: What It Is, What It Isn't, and How to Get Your Life Back*, Ramsey Press, 2020.

de Waal, Frans. *The Age of Empathy: Nature's Lessons for a Kinder Society*, Crown, 2010.

Elle, Alexandra. *How We Heal: Uncover Your Power and Set Yourself Free*, Chronicle Books, 2022.

Headlee, Celeste. *We Need to Talk: How to Have Conversations that Matter*, Harper Collins, 2017.

Hood, Bruce. *The Science of Happiness: Seven Lessons for Living Well*, Simon & Schuster, 2024.

Keltner, Dacher. *Awe: The New Science of Everyday Wonder and How It Can Transform Your Life*, Penguin Books, 2024.

Krznaric, Roman. *Empathy: Why It Matters, and How to Get It*, TarcherPerigee, 2015.

Lowery, Brian, PhD. *Selfless: The Social Creation of "You,"* Harper Collins, 2023.

McLaren, Karla. *The Art of Empathy: A Complete Guide to Life's Most Essential Skill*, Sounds True Adult, 2013.

Orloff, Judith, MD. *The Empath's Survival Guide: Life Strategies for Sensitive People*, Sounds True Adult, 2018.

—. *The Genius of Empathy: Practical Skills to Heal Your Sensitive Self, Your Relationships & the World*, Sounds True, 2024.

Orsillo, Susan M., PhD, and Lizabeth Roemer, PhD. *The Mindful Way through Anxiety: Break Free from Chronic Worry and Reclaim Your Life*, The Guilford Press, 2011.

"Putting Feelings into Words: Affect Labeling as Implicit Emotion Regulation," *Emotion Review*, Sage Journals, Volume 10, Issue 2 (3/2018).

Rymsha, Charlene. *Burn Bright: Heal Yourself from Burnout and Live with Presence, Purpose & Peace*, Rock Point, 2021.

Schwartz, Kristen. *The Healed Empath: The Highly Sensitive Person's Guide to Transforming Trauma and Anxiety, Trusting Your Intuition, and Moving from Overwhelming to Empowerment*, Fair Winds Press, 2022.

Snow, April. *Find Your Strength: A Workbook for the Highly Sensitive Person*, Wellfleet Press, 2022.

Tawwab, Nedra Glover. *Set Boundaries, Find Peace: A Guide to Reclaiming Yourself*, TarcherPerigee, 2021.

Viscott, David, MD. *Emotional Resilience: Simple Truths for Dealing with the Unfinished Business of Your Past*, Three Rivers Press, 1996.

ABOUT THE AUTHOR

Susan Reynolds has written, co-authored, or edited more than 25 nonfiction books, primarily self-help works on everything from finance to meditation to neuroscience. Her books include *Finding Your Authentic Self*, *5-Minute Productivity Workbook*, *Fire Up Your Writing Brain*, and *Train Your Brain to Get Happy*. She writes blogs for Psychologytoday.com and on fireupyourwritingbrain.com.